Contents

Introduction 2
The game 3
  The pitch 4
  The goal 6
  The penalty spot 7
  The striking circle 7
  Other lines 7
Equipment 8
  The stick 8
  Ball 9
  Uniform 9
  Goalkeeper's equipment 9
  The umpires 9
Playing the game 11
  Timing 11
  General rule 11
  To start a half and
    restart after a goal 11
  Open play 12
  Ball out of play 12

  Scoring a goal 13
  Bully 13
  The raised ball 14
  Defending shots at goal 14
  Handling the ball 16
  Foot–ball contact 16
Penalties 17
  Match penalties 17
  Procedure for match penalties 18
  Personal penalties 22
  Procedure for personal penalties 22
Control of the game 24
  Umpires 24
  Match officials 25
Understanding the game 26
  Phases of the game 26
  Grip 29
  Footwork 29
  Vision 29

Attacking play 30
  Controlling the ball 30
  Running with the ball 30
  Dribbling 31
  Dodging 31
  Passing 32
  Receiving the ball 34
  Shooting and goal-scoring 34
Defending play 35
  Intercepting 35
  Tackling 35
  Marking 38
  Goalkeeping 40
Restarts and set pieces 42
  Free hits 42
  Hits-in from the side line 43
  Hits-in from a corner 43
  Penalty corners 43
Metric conversion table 47
Index 48

Acknowledgements

Photographs on front and back cover and pages 2, 3, 8, 28 and 30 courtesy of Empics; photographs on inside front cover and pages 5, 7, 10, 15, 19, 37, 42, 46 and 47 courtesy of Allsport UK Ltd; photographs on pages 16, 21, 31, 32, 41 and inside back cover courtesy of English Hockey.

Illustrations on pages 4, 6, 25, 27, 38, 39, 43, 44 and 45 by Dave Saunders; all other illustrations by Ron Dixon.

Note Throughout the book players and officials are referred to individually as 'he'. This should, of course, be taken to mean 'he or she' where appropriate. All measurements are given in imperial units; a metric conversion table is given on page 47.

Introduction

Hockey, known in Canada and the USA as field hockey, is an international sport governed by the Federation Internationale de Hockey (FIH). This book sets out the general form and conduct of the game; detailed reference can also be sought from the *Rules of Hockey*, published annually by the Hockey Rules Board and obtainable from English Hockey. Importantly, the *Rules* also include the Interpretations, which are in turn amplified as required on both the FIH and the English Hockey websites.

For the English Hockey website, see: www.hockeyonline.co.uk

The game

Hockey is played by two teams, each comprising up to 16 players, of whom a maximum of 11 may be on the pitch at any one time and one of whom must be a properly equipped goalkeeper. Each team must have a captain, who is recognised by the wearing of an armband. The captain is responsible for the proper conduct of their team.

Each team defends its own half of the field, the captains having tossed a coin to determine either possession of the ball to start the game or which end to defend, and changes end after half-time. The team that did not have possession to start the game has possession to start the second half.

The remaining five players may be used as substitutes and brought on to the field at any time except when a penalty corner is awarded and during its progress. All substitutions on and off the field take place at the halfway line. Exceptionally, a defending goalkeeper who is injured or suspended when a penalty corner is awarded or during its taking may be substituted, as the game cannot be played without a goalkeeper on the field for each side. The team captains are responsible for ensuring that substitution is carried out correctly, though in some games team officials, usually the manager or the coach, handle this.

The aim of the game is to score goals by the attacking team's playing the ball with the stick into the goal from inside a limited area known as the striking circle. Therefore, unlike some other sports, a defending team cannot score an 'own goal'.

The pitch

A hockey pitch may be of grass, all-weather surface or of artificial turf with either a sand or water base. The number of artificial pitches is increasing, not least because they make it easier for inexperienced players to play and enjoy the game, and hence improve its speed and quality and the predictability of the ball's behaviour. In England most pitches were and remain marked in imperial measurements; both imperial and metric are therefore given in this book.

The pitch is 100 yds (91.4 m) long by 60 yds (55 m) wide and is split across its width into four equal-sized quarters by continuous lines. A flag on a post 4–5 ft (1.2–1.5 m) high is placed at each corner. All lines are 3 in (75 mm) wide.

In club games, the host team captain has the responsibility for ensuring that the pitch and its furniture are safe and in good condition (especially the goal nets) and that, if necessary, proper arrangements are made for the control of spectators. At higher levels, separately appointed match officials usually assume these additional responsibilities.

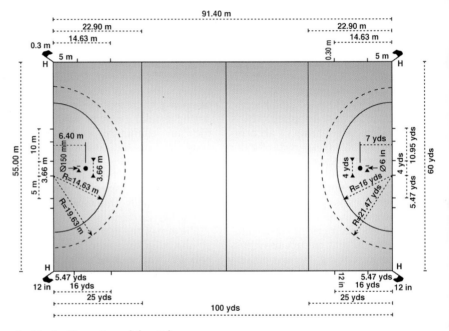

▲ *Fig. 1 Dimensions of the pitch*

4

The goal

At the centre of and on the outer edge of each backline is placed the goal. This is rectangular, painted white, and is 12 ft (3.66 m) wide by 7 ft (2.14 m) high on the inside measurements of the posts. The uprights and crossbar are 2 in (51 mm) wide by 3 in (75 mm) deep. On their back edges is fixed the goal net which is in turn attached to the back and side boards 18 in (46 cm) high, the side boards being at least 4 ft (1.2 m) long. The part of the backline between the goal uprights is known as the goal line.

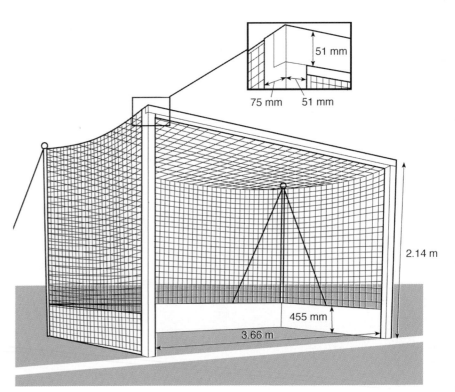

▶ *Fig. 2 Dimensions of the goal*

The penalty spot

In front of the centre of each goal is a spot, known as the penalty spot, 6 in (150 mm) in diameter and 7 yds (64 cm) in front of the inner edge of the goal line.

The striking circle

In front of each goal line is a straight line 3.66 m wide, positioned such that its furthest edge is 16 yds (14.63 m) from and parallel to the goal line. Each edge is then joined to the backline by a quarter circle. The area enclosed within these lines, i.e. by the lines themselves and the area within them, is known as the striking circle. In addition, broken lines 5 m from the outer edge of the circle are marked, starting from the centre of the top of the circle. These lines, at the time of writing, are mandatory for international matches, but pitches may otherwise be marked with imperial markings as required by English Hockey or until mandated otherwise by the FIH.

Other lines

On 'old' pitches, short lines 1 ft (30 cm) long are marked at 5 and 10 yds from the goalposts on the inner edge of the backline. On newer pitches marked metrically, these lines are 30 cm long but marked on the outer edge of the backline, 5 and 10 m from the goalposts. Similar lines are marked on the sidelines 5 yds (inside the pitch) or 5 m (outside the pitch) from the corner flags, and also on the sideline in line with the top of the circle.

Equipment

The stick

The stick is made of wood or any material containing wood, but may not contain metal. Its weight and dimensions are determined by the *Rules of Hockey*. It is crooked at the lower end with a flat side on the left of the hook. That flat side and the part of the stick above it, together with its edges, are the permitted playing surfaces of the stick. The back of the stick is not permitted for playing the ball. Sticks are normally straight from the top of the handle to the beginning of the crook, but some sideways deviation from this is permitted. 'Left-handed' sticks are not permitted. Sand-based pitches tend to wear sticks very badly, so umpires check that sticks are safe to play with, especially with respect to chipped and splintered stick-heads. The use of tapes and resins to repair the sticks is permitted. It is each player's responsibility to use a stick that is safe and compliant with the rules.

Ball

The ball is round, hard, may be made of any material, is usually covered in plastic, and may be coloured white or any other suitable colour; it is noted that colour-blind players and umpires normally prefer the use of a white ball. *The Rules* specify the ball's weight and dimensions, which are similar to those of a cricket ball.

Uniform

Teams are required to dress in their proper colours, with the shorts and socks of each team being a different colour to those of the opposing team. There is no mandatory requirement for players to wear footwear, shin-pads or mouth-guards, but they may *not* wear hats with sharp peaks or jewellery that might injure other players. It is a normal requirement of competitive hockey that players be clearly numbered on the backs of their shirts, and that players retain their published numbers should a change of shirt colour be required for a match.

Goalkeeper's equipment

Goalkeepers must wear a full helmet and a shirt of a different colour to those of either team. The goalkeeper's shirt must be numbered on both front and back. Other equipment for goalkeepers is optional but normally includes kickers, leg guards, thigh and chest padding under the shirt, and gloves/hand protectors. The goalkeeper must wear the helmet throughout the game, but is exceptionally permitted to remove it when taking (not defending) a penalty stroke.

The umpires

Umpires should carry:

- a current rule book
- a whistle
- a stop watch
- a pencil and card on which to record the score, and any players cautioned, warned or suspended
- misconduct cards (*see* page 22).

The umpires are a team, just as the players are in teams. They should therefore be similarly dressed in shirts of the same colour and with black trousers/skirts and socks of the same colour. The wearing of peaked hats should normally be restricted to keeping rain or sun out of the eyes, so that their faces can be seen at all times.

Playing the game

Timing

The game consists of two 35-minute periods separated by a half-time period of 5 to 10 minutes, with the teams changing ends at half-time. Half-time might need to be extended to allow for watering of water-based pitches; this should normally be determined before the game starts. In some competitions, a game drawn at full-time may require the playing of extra time, which will normally start after a 5-minute break and consist of two 7½-minute periods separated by a 3-minute interval, the captains having tossed for possession or end to start the period. It is not unusual for this extra time to be terminated as soon as a goal is scored – the 'golden goal'. In continuation, if no goal is scored during extra time, a match will usually proceed to a penalty stroke competition (see *Rules of Hockey*).

General rule

Whenever a team is awarded exclusive possession of the ball, e.g. to start each half, to put the ball back into play or to take a free hit or penalty corner, all members of the opposing team *must* be at least 5 m away. For all such events, the ball must be stationary and the player playing the ball must not intentionally raise it from the ground nor play it dangerously or so as to be likely to cause danger, though accidental raising of the ball may be permitted if no danger ensues. The player must move the ball at least 1 m before any other player of the same side may play it. In all cases, the ball may be pushed or hit. After taking the stroke, the player may not approach or remain within playing distance of the ball until another player of either side has played it.

To start a half and restart after a goal

Teams must be in their own half of the pitch. When the umpire blows the whistle, the ball may be pushed or hit in any direction by a player of the team that did not choose ends. After half-time, a player of the opposing team restarts in similar fashion. After a goal, the game is restarted by the umpire who awarded the goal by the team against which the goal was scored/awarded. Time is *not* stopped when a goal is awarded.

Open play

In open play, players may hit, flick, scoop or push the ball in any direction, and raise it to any height, provided they do not directly endanger other players or cause them to play dangerously, e.g. by raising their sticks above their shoulders to play an aerial ball.

Given that hockey is, in essence, a non-contact sport, they may tackle for the ball with their sticks from any direction but may not intentionally make physical contact with each other or with each other's sticks. Physical contact is, however, inevitable, given the speed of the game. Umpires will therefore be seeking to ensure that the ball is played properly before any other contact between sticks and/or bodies is made. Intentional physical contact, e.g. pushing, pulling, barging or hitting of sticks, is severely detrimental to the game and can lead to personal confrontations. It should normally be penalised with both a match penalty and a personal penalty (see pages 17–23).

In this respect, the obstruction rule plays a major part. Players may not shield the ball with their sticks or bodies when being tackled. A tackling player must therefore be in the right **Position**, displaying **Intent** to play the ball, i.e. with the stick on or near the ground, and use proper **Timing** when using the stick to approach the ball – this is known as **PIT**. It is clear, therefore, that both the ball's possessor and potential tackler have a duty of care for each other and that they comply with the *Rules'* requirements. To **PIT** may be added **S**, for **Speed**. Either player in a tackling situation may add **Speed** to the equation, either by passing or moving quickly away with the ball when a tackle is likely or, in the case of the tackler, by using a quick stab of the stick to play the ball away from its possessor.

Ball out of play

The ball may be sent out of play over either the sideline or the backline by either team.

- **Sideline.** If the ball goes over the sideline, it or another ball is placed on the line where it left the pitch and a player of the team that did not put the ball out of play may hit or push it, as outlined previously.

- **Backline, by an attacker.** The ball is placed on the ground opposite to where it went over the backline and up to 16 yds (14.63 m) from the backline, and hit or pushed into play by a defender.

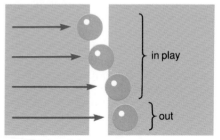

▲ *Fig. 3 Ball in and out of play*

- **Backline including the goal line, _unintentionally_ by a defender.** The ball is placed on the corner mark on the sideline on whichever side of the goal the ball left the pitch and hit or pushed into play by a player of the attacking side.
- **Backline or goal line, _intentionally_ by a defender** (if no goal is scored). A penalty corner is awarded against the defending team. Note that, in this case, a goal might be scored had the ball been played in the circle by an attacker without previously having gone outside the circle.

Umpires need to be particularly careful when determining whether a ball is sent out of play intentionally by defenders, especially by goalkeepers. As a general guide, if a goalkeeper uses the foot nearest the backline to clear the ball and it goes out of play, it may be unintentional, but use of the foot furthest from the backline usually, though not necessarily, indicates intent.

Scoring a goal

For a goal to be scored, the ball must be played by an attacker within the circle and pass _completely_ over the goal line, and for this purpose it should be noted that the lines delineating the circle form part of it. It does not matter if the ball is subsequently played by or safely touches any part of the body of a defender; provided it does not leave the circle, a goal is still scored. If the ball _does_ leave the circle, it must again be played in the circle by an attacker before entering the goal. Special rules apply to penalty corners and penalty strokes.

Bully

If a bully is awarded, one player of each side faces the other and the opposite sideline, each with their own goal to the right, with the ball on the ground between them and all other players of both sides at least 5 m away. When the whistle is blown to start the bully, each player taps their opponent's stick with their stick above the ball, then taps the ground to the right of the ball, alternately, three times, and may then play the ball.

A bully may be awarded if, for example, the ball becomes trapped in a player's clothing (though not a goalkeeper's), if it disintegrates during play, if there is a simultaneous breach of the _Rules_ necessitating a stoppage of play, or an injury where no penalty is awarded. A bully may not be played within 16 yds (14.63 m) of the backline.

The raised ball

In open play, the ball may be raised by any means to any height, provided it is neither dangerous in itself nor likely to lead to danger. Such raising of the ball may be done by flicking or scooping it. It is not permitted for the ball to be intentionally raised from an award for an event, e.g free hit, hit-in for ball out of play, corner. The ball may not be lofted so as to drop into the circle, though it may be raised, if safe, enough to overcome a potential tackle. Equally, from a free hit, corner or a hit-in, the ball might be permitted to enter the circle whilst in the air, provided it was raised accidentally and is safe in itself and unlikely to lead to dangerous play.

Scooping of the ball is one of the means of making the ball travel a long distance over the heads of and beyond a defence. It is imperative that the ball be safe on the way up and that only one player of either side receives it and plays it safely to the ground before any opponent may approach within playing distance. If players of both sides are likely to be beneath the ball when it descends, a penalty is awarded against the team that raised the ball from where it was first played. If, on the other hand, a player of either side receives or is about to receive the ball but is hindered by the proximity of an opponent, a penalty is awarded against that opponent where the ball lands.

At no time may any player except a goalkeeper play or attempt to play a ball above shoulder height. The goalkeeper in that instance may stop or deflect such a ball with hand or stick, but not propel it.

Players may not raise the ball off the ground and then hit it whilst it is in the air. This can be dangerous and should be penalised by the umpires.

Special rules apply to the raising of the ball at a penalty corner.

Defending shots at goal

Goalkeepers

A goalkeeper may legitimately stand or adopt any necessary posture to defend shots at goal, including lying on the ground ('logging'). Any part of the body may be used to stop a shot. The legs, feet and stick may be used to propel the ball except that, for a ball above the shoulder, the stick may be used only to deflect or stop the ball, not to propel it. Other parts of the body, especially the hand not holding the stick, may be used to stop but *not* to propel the ball. The goalkeeper may deflect the ball over the crossbar or round the uprights by use of hand or stick.

Other defenders

Defenders other than goalkeepers have no special privileges when it comes to defending against goals. If they elect to stand in the goal, thus to act as goalkeeper, when the ball is on its way into the goal, and use any part of their

bodies to stop or propel the ball, or use their sticks to stop or propel the ball approaching above shoulder height, and thus prevent a goal, a penalty stroke will be awarded against them.

Ball in goalkeeper's clothing

If the ball becomes lodged in the goalkeeper's clothing in the circle, a penalty corner should be awarded. Note that the award would be a bully were the ball to lodge in any other player's clothing.

Handling the ball

Only goalkeepers are permitted to handle the ball. However, a player may use the hand in self-defence for a ball likely to strike the body. In such a case, the player concerned would not be penalised, though a penalty might need to be awarded against the player who raised the ball in the first place.

Foot–ball contact

If the ball strikes the foot or any other part of a player's body, there is no offence provided the player could not avoid the contact. Only if the player gains a major advantage would a penalty normally be applied. However, when the body, usually the foot, strikes the ball, that is an offence as only the stick may be used to play the ball, so a penalty may be applied against that player or team.

Penalties

There are two forms of penalty in hockey – the match penalty, of which there are six, and the personal penalty, of which there are four.

Match penalties

Free hit

This is the normal penalty for a basic offence, such as kicking the ball, raising the ball dangerously, barging, etc. It is a hit or push awarded by the umpire to the team against which the offence has occurred. A free hit can be awarded to either team anywhere on the pitch except when a defending team commits an offence in its own circle.

Advance 10 metres

The umpire directs that the free hit may be advanced 10 m for a further offence by the previously offending side, such as intentionally remaining within 5 m of the hit's position, showing dissent about the award or picking up the ball so as to delay the hit. There is no compulsion for the ball to be advanced, but if such an advance would then take the free hit into the opposing circle, the award must be increased to a penalty corner.

Reverse the free hit

The umpire reverses the award so that the originally offending team is awarded the free hit. Examples might be the striker, having hit the ball poorly, remaining within 1 m of it when an opponent attempts to play it, or delaying the hit so as to allow other players of the team to gain better positions.

Penalty corner

Awarded against a defending team:

- that commits an intentional offence within its own 25 yd (23 m) area but outside the circle. This may be accompanied by some form of personal penalty
- for an unintentional offence inside its own circle that does not prevent a possible goal nor denies an attacker actual or likely possession of the ball
- for an intentional offence by a defender inside the circle against an opponent not in possession or likely to gain possession of the ball. This award must be accompanied by some form of personal penalty for misconduct.

Penalty stroke

This is awarded for:

- persistent breaking of the backline by the defenders at a penalty corner
- an intentional breach by the defence that prevents a goal being scored or to deprive an attacker of actual or likely possession of the ball

- an unintentional breach by the defence that prevents a probable goal.

Application of advantage

This is when the umpire intentionally refrains from blowing the whistle for an offence, but instead signals for play to proceed and may indeed call the players to play on. Its object is to minimise any profit to a team that has committed an offence, usually by leaving the opponents in possession of the ball. In effect, the umpire will be seeking to impose at least as great a penalty by not blowing as might have been effected had the whistle been blown. An alternative way of looking at it is to consider what the offending team's captain would *least* like the umpire to do.

The application of advantage can apply to all the normal match penalties. It also underlines the need for umpires not to be hasty in blowing the whistle. Play can often be allowed to proceed and then, dependent on the outcome, a decision made as to whether or not to ignore the previous offence or bring play to a halt and award the appropriate match penalty where the offence occurred.

Signalling advantage is important in every case not only for distant players to continue positional play, but also so that the umpire's colleague is aware of what is happening, thus avoiding unnecessary intervention.

Procedure for match penalties

Free hit

The umpire blows the whistle and raises an arm with palm outstretched, at shoulder height, in the direction of the hit. The hit or push is taken on or near the spot where the offence took place with minimum delay. Players of the opposing team should be at least 5 m away. Exceptionally, for a free hit awarded to the attacking team within 5 m of the circle, all players of both teams, other than the striker, must be at least 5 m from the ball. If the attackers infringe, a free hit is awarded to the defence and, if the defence infringes, a penalty corner is awarded.

Advance 10 metres

The umpire blows the whistle and holds up an arm above the head, with fist clenched. The team taking the free hit may move the ball forwards for up to 10 m.

Reverse the free hit

The umpire blows the whistle and indicates in the opposite direction to the original free hit. Such an award would normally be accompanied by the umpire's indicating why the decision is reversed.

Penalty corner

(a) The umpire blows the whistle and holds both arms straight in front of the body, pointing towards the goal and with palms facing each other, while looking at the players concerned, not the goal.
(b) Up to five defenders move behind their backline and the remainder beyond the centre line.
(c) The supporting umpire moves into the control umpire's half so as to control

the halfway line and offer support to the controlling umpire.

(d) The ball is placed on or beyond the 10 yd (10 m) line on the backline.

(e) Defenders behind the backline remain at least 5 yds (5 m) clear of the ball.

(f) An attacker takes position to inject the ball, having at least one foot outside the field.

(g) The remaining attackers, who can be all except their goalkeeper, take position outside the circle. They may be within the 5 m dotted line, however.

(h) When ready, the attacker on the backline hits or pushes the ball. No goal can be scored from this initial propulsion.

(i) When the ball is moved, the defenders may leave the backline and the attackers may enter the circle. If the defenders move too early and gain advantage, the penalty corner may be ordered to be taken again or, if this breaking is persistent, a penalty stroke may be awarded. If the attackers move too early, a free hit is awarded to the defence.

(j) The ball may be played by either or both teams outside the circle but must be stopped or come to rest on the ground outside the circle before any attempt to shoot at goal from inside the circle can be made.

(k) If the first shot at goal is a *hit* the ball must cross the goal line or be on a path that would take it across the goal line, before any deflection by any player, at a height not exceeding 18 in (46 cm) – the height of the backboard, unless it touches the stick or person of a defender during its travel. The important emphasis here is on the safety of the shot. A ball may loop higher than the indicated height during its travel, but it is its height as it crosses the goal line that matters.

(l) For any other type of shot at goal, and for subsequent hits, the ball may be raised to any height, subject to there being no actual or caused danger.

(m) A defender other than the goalkeeper who remains in the goal to defend it and whose body stops the ball from entering the goal should be penalised with a penalty stroke.

(n) If the ball travels beyond 5 yds (5 m) from the circle, i.e. beyond the 5 m dotted line if marked, the penalty corner is ended.

(o) If time for a half completes on the award of or during the taking of a penalty corner, the penalty must be completed unless another penalty corner or a penalty stroke is awarded, in which case that must be completed. In addition to the normal reasons for ending a penalty corner, the penalty in this particular case ends if the ball passes out of the circle for a second time.

The penalty stroke

(a) The umpire blows the whistle, raises one arm vertically and points to the penalty spot with the other.

(b) Time is stopped by both umpires and, if required, by match officials.

(c) The goalkeeper moves to take up position with both feet on the goal line. Provided some part of the foot is on the line, it does not matter whether it is the toes, heels or the whole foot.

(d) The support umpire, having checked where non-participating players are, takes up position on the backline some 10 m from goal.

(e) The control umpire takes up position behind and slightly to the right of the striker.

(f) The striker, who may be the attacking team's goalkeeper, places the ball on the penalty spot and takes up position behind the ball, ready to shoot. If the striker is the other goalkeeper, the helmet and gloves may be removed.

(g) All non-participating players retire beyond the 25 yd (23 m) line.

(h) The controlling umpire checks with the striker and the goalkeeper that each is ready to start.

(i) The control umpire blows the whistle to start the stroke.

(j) The striker may push, flick or scoop the ball, touching it once only, to any height towards goal. The ball may *not* be hit, nor may the striker feint at playing the ball.

(k) The striker may take one step forward. The rear foot may not pass the front one until the ball has been played.

(l) If the ball is pushed, it may not be dragged.

(m) If the ball goes into goal, the umpire blows the whistle and signals a goal and the teams move into their own halves ready for the game to restart.

(n) If a goal is not scored, the ball comes to rest inside the circle, is caught in the goalkeeper's leg-guard, is caught by the goalkeeper, passes outside the circle, or if the stroke-taker breaches a *Rule*, the umpire blows the whistle to end the stroke and the teams prepare for the game to restart with a defensive hit 16 yds (14.63 m) in front of the centre of the goal line.

(o) If the defending goalkeeper breaches any rule that prevents a goal from being scored, the umpire blows the whistle and awards a penalty goal. The teams then take up position to restart the game from the centre line.

(p) When both umpires and the teams are in position either in their own halves if a goal was scored or awarded or to restart with a hit in front of the circle, the controlling umpire blows the whistle to restart the clocks and the game.

Personal penalties

Personal penalties are used to deal with misconduct by players, and will nearly always follow a match penalty, though not necessarily at the time if advantage is played. They take the form of a caution, a warning (green card awarded), a temporary suspension (yellow card awarded) and permanent suspension (red card awarded).

Procedure for personal penalties

Rough or dangerous play, a captain's not properly exercising responsibilities for the team's conduct, or any other form of misconduct, should be dealt with by a match penalty if appropriate and may also be awarded a personal penalty. A personal penalty might not necessarily be awarded at the time of an offence but rather at the first available stoppage if application of advantage can safely allow play to proceed. The use of green, yellow and red cards is advisable if they are available, but not mandatory. A player who has been awarded a warning or temporary suspension for a specific offence may not be awarded the same personal penalty for a repetition of that offence.

Caution

A caution will normally take the form of a brief address by the umpire to the player concerned. It may be used without necessarily stopping the game. It could simply take the form of a loud whistle and a warning sign, accompanied by a clearly visual facial expression from the umpire. A caution might also be given to a team captain to exercise responsibility more effectively. If this is done, the game should be stopped so that the umpire can address the captain and then time given to the captain, or both captains if need be, to put the message to their teams.

Warning

A warning should normally be accompanied by the award of a green card to the player or players concerned. To do this, the game should be stopped and, if necessary, a check made with match officials that they can see what is happening. The offending player(s) should be called to stand in front of the umpire who may then indicate verbally what the award is for. The umpire should write down the time of the event, the number(s) of the player(s) concerned and a brief note of the reason. When this is done, the player(s) should be invited to turn so that the umpire's colleague and match official, if present, can also see the number(s) and record the event. On completion, the offending player(s) may be returned to their positions and the match restarted. It is important that umpires should not rush this procedure, not least because it gives time for players to regain their composure.

Temporary suspension

A temporary suspension should be for a minimum of 5 minutes and normally accompanied by the award of a yellow card. A suspended player should usually be sent under the care of a match official, if one is appointed, or to the corner of the pitch by the nearer umpire at the player's defending end. Whilst under suspension, the player should remain silent but may be taken water and protective clothing. If silence is not observed, or if there is continuing misconduct, the suspension may be lengthened. Putting suspended players behind their goals may place them at risk from balls rebounding off fencing behind the goals. Sending them to their team benches, unless under the care of a match official, risks the umpires' losing sight of the offender and that player then being used as a substitute. It is a courtesy to indicate to the umpire's colleague and the offender's team captain the proposed length of the suspension. On completion of temporary suspension, the team may nominate a substitute rather than the offender to return to the pitch.

Permanent suspension

This would be used by the umpire to deal with a particularly unpleasant offence, often one involving some form of personal violence. It is indicated by the use of a red card. The suspended player is required immediately to be completely removed from the pitch and may not re-enter it throughout the duration of the game. In England, such offences are covered by the National Disciplinary Code, which requires that the player be automatically suspended from playing, coaching or umpiring for a minimum period of 16 days. The Code makes provision for extended suspension dependent on the nature of the offence and is itself dependent on the umpires' filling in and rendering a red card report form.

Suspension of goalkeepers

If a goalkeeper is suspended, and given that the game cannot proceed without a goalkeeper of each team on the pitch, a substitute goalkeeper must be provided. If a properly-equipped substitute goalkeeper is on the substitutes' bench, that goalkeeper may be used and a field player removed from the pitch for the duration of the suspension in that game. If no substitute goalkeeper is available, a field player will need to be given time to don goalkeeping equipment and act as goalkeeper for the duration of the suspension in that game. That equipment might, in the circumstances, be limited to a helmet and a shirt of a colour different from those worn by the teams. Such a player must keep the helmet on even when playing outside the circle, but must be very circumspect so as not to endanger other players.

Control of the game

Umpires

Two umpires are appointed to a match. Each has prime though not exclusive responsibility for the proper conduct of play in the half with the nearer goal to the right and has jurisdiction over all the players and other team members. They thus operate on opposite sides of the pitch and do *not* change ends at half-time. They time the match with stopwatches, unless that duty has been assumed by separate match officials, and ensure that a penalty corner in progress when a half ends is completed. They keep written records of goals scored/awarded and of players cautioned, warned or suspended. They each have exclusive responsibility for the award and control of corners, penalty corners, penalty strokes and goals in their own ends and circles.

Umpiring decisions to start and stop the game for any reason, to award goals and match penalties are indicated by the blowing of the whistle and the appropriate signal. They also signal, when the ball goes out of play, on the method of restarting the game, though do not necessarily need to whistle for this.

Importantly, the umpires act as a team. They normally meet well before the game to determine their umpiring strategy as well as to carry out normal aerobic and non-aerobic match preparation and often assist the host team's captain in tending poor goal nets. Throughout the game they work together, signalling to each other, e.g. when applying advantage, and also when asked for help. An umpire may *not* award a penalty corner, penalty stroke or goal in the other half of the pitch but may assist in the making of that decision if asked to do so by the other umpire.

Although main umpiring responsibility is within each half, in normal practice an umpire's control area is from the far edge of the inner circle diagonally to the near edge of the other umpire's circle. Within those areas, the umpires normally expect to deal with incidents in which the ball is coming towards their own end.

It is also important that the umpires be fully fit and capable of umpiring at the level of the match. At higher levels of hockey, umpires are required to pass a bleep test every season to ensure their continuing fitness. They must be flexible – able to run not only forwards but also sideways and backwards, thus to maintain constant full vision of the pitch and of their colleagues. Above all, they must concentrate hard throughout the whole 4,200 seconds of the game, be brisk and purposeful in their movements and confident in their physical presentation of decisions.

Umpires are encouraged to give their signals clearly, at head height, and to whistle once for every event but to vary the tone/length of the whistle blast according to the nature of that event. For example, a brief blow of the whistle would suffice for a minor technical offence, whereas a long, hard blow might be necessary to deal with a more serious offence where the umpire wishes to display displeasure and a warning not to repeat the offence.

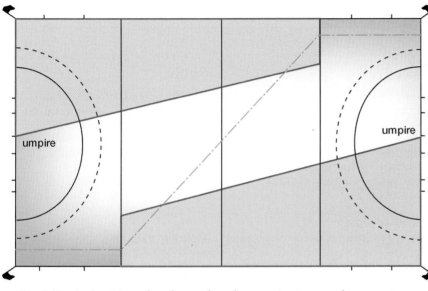

▲ *Fig. 4 Umpires' positions: the red areas show the approximate range of movement; the blue lines, the division of responsibility*

Umpires should not normally indicate which end each will take until the team captains have made their decision.

Match officials

An independent match official may be appointed to higher level games and, in tournaments, a tournament director with technical officers and judges. Their duties include the checking of team lists, pre-match checking of players' equipment, recording of all match events, timing of the match and general liaison with the local personnel for spectator control, pitch watering, etc. A reserve umpire might also be appointed, who should mentally umpire the whole match and record all incidents – when, who, what and why, so as to be ready at a moment's notice to take over from one of the umpires. Match officials can be of great help to umpires, so it is important that they and the umpires work together as a team.

Understanding the game

To the casual observer, hockey can sometimes appear complex. In fact, it is an exceedingly simple game once the basic concepts, skills and rules have been learnt and understood.

Phases of the game

There are two distinct phases in a game of hockey:

- the attacking phase – when one's own team has the ball, and
- the defending phase – when the opposition has the ball.

The objectives, for both the individual and the team, for each phase are as follows.

Objectives

Attacking phase
- To keep possession.
- To move the ball forwards and penetrate the opposing defence at the earliest opportunity.
- To create shooting and goal-scoring opportunities in the opposing circle.
- To score goals.

Defending phase
- To regain possession at the earliest opportunity.
- To prevent the ball being played or carried forwards, i.e. to prevent the opposition penetrating one's own defence.
- To deny the opposition shooting and goal-scoring opportunities in one's own circle.
- To avoid conceding goals.

The following skills are required to achieve the objectives in each phase.

Skills

Attacking phase
- Control of and composure on the ball.
- Ability to run with the ball.
- Ability to dribble and dodge.
- Ability to pass.
- Ability to receive a pass.
- Ability to create and convert goal-scoring opportunities.

Defending phase
- Ability to mark.
- Ability to delay, channel and close down opponents.
- Ability to intercept and tackle.
- Ability to prevent and deny shooting/goal-scoring opportunities.
- Ability to protect and defend the goal – effective goalkeeping.

The styles of play demanded during each of these phases can be described as follows.

- Attacking phase – fluid, expansive and creative.
- Defending phase – disciplined, organised and secure.

In similar fashion, the game's principles of play are determined by these two phases.

- In attack – possession, speed, support, penetration, concentration, width and mobility.
- In defence – depth, delay, balance, concentration, organisation, security and speed.

To perform effectively in the game, players must have a full understanding of the objectives, styles and principles of play required of them during the different phases of the game and in the different areas of the pitch. Most importantly, effective team play is dependent on individual players mastering and performing the basic techniques and skills.

Zonal priorities

Fig. 5 depicts the zonal priorities on the field.

- Attacking zone – speed, penetration and creativity.
- Build-up/consolidation zone – possession, control, deception and construction.
- Defending zone – discipline, safety and organisation.

There are three basic factors which underpin the skills of the game.

- Grip.
- Footwork.
- Vision.

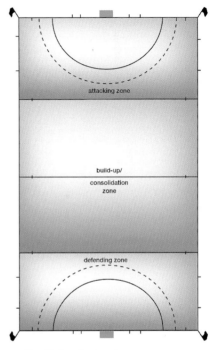

▲ *Fig. 5 Zonal priorities*

Grip

Mastery of the grip is an important element in the acquisition and execution of all skills. Methods of employing the correct grip should be introduced early in the development process.

The left hand holds the top of the stick so that a 'V' is formed by the thumb and forefinger down the back of the stick. This grip will result in the flat (hitting) face of the stick facing the ground. The right hand should be placed a third to halfway down the shaft of the stick. The rotational movement of the stick from open to reverse stick and back is controlled by the left hand, while the right hand provides added support and control as the stick is rotated through it. Some players prefer to extend the index finger of the right hand down the shaft of the stick to further aid control, however young players should not be encouraged to do this for safety reasons. Both hands must feel comfortable when the stick is held in the open and reverse stick position.

▲ *Fig. 6 Gripping the stick*

Footwork

Players must learn to move forwards, sideways and backwards while maintaining close contact of the ball. Good footwork will increase a player's mobility and is essential in creating space and time when under pressure.

Vision

When in control of the ball, a player must be able to see as much as possible of what is occuring over the rest of the pitch. The position in which the ball is controlled and carried in relation to the body will assist or restrict vision. If the ball is held in front of and slightly to the right of the body with the upper body inclined forwards, the player will have good vision of what is happening around him. If the ball is kept too close to the feet, the player's body will inevitably be bent over the ball and his vision reduced accordingly.

It is essential to ensure that in developing close control, vision and awareness are not impaired or restricted.

Attacking play

Controlling the ball

Control and composure are essential when players are attempting to retain possession of the ball in the game, especially when being pressured and harassed by opponents intent on dispossessing them.

Practices which allow players to keep, manipulate, juggle and manoeuvre the ball with the stick will develop control, confidence and composure on the ball.

Running with the ball

Running with the ball encompasses a number of techniques and requires the player to 'carry' or propel the ball with the stick, but without any exaggerated or complex movement of stick and ball. This should permit them to look up and assess the situation before choosing the next move.

Running with the ball is most effective when there is plenty of time and space to operate and where there are no opponents in close proximity; it can be used also to run past and beat an opponent if necessary.

Technique

- Hold the body as near upright as possible, holding the stick at the top with the left hand.
- The stick and ball should be kept well out in front of the body and slightly to the right, so making it easier to run at speed and to look up while doing so.
- Good balanced footwork is essential, as is the ability to 'scan' ahead to read the pattern of play. Players must learn to recognise when they should pass and when they should run with the ball. Both skills require close control.

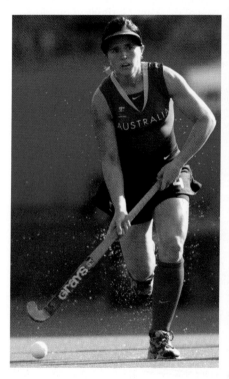

Dribbling

The (Indian) dribble forms the basis of all stickwork. Once mastered, it allows a player to move to the more complex skills of feinting, dodging, 'dummying' and eliminating opponents.

Technique

- When employing this skill, the ball is tapped and dragged from left to right with a rolling action of the hands and wrists.
- It is the left hand that controls the twisting, rotational movement of the stick while the right hand generates the pulling and pushing action necessary for moving the ball. The right hand also provides the control and stability for action.
- Young players should first learn to move the ball from open to reverse stick and back again while stationary. Once this has been mastered, the skill can be attempted at walking, then jogging and eventually running speed.

Dodging

Dodging is performed by combining and co-ordinating the movements of body, stick and ball. The object at all times is to give the impression that you are moving in a certain direction, then suddenly, when the opponent is committed to covering the first move, you change direction and move past the opponent on the other side.

Although some considerable time should be devoted to acquiring the techniques and skills required for beating an opponent in one-to-one situations, it must be stressed that still the best way to beat an opponent is to pass the ball around or past him.

Passing

Passing is often described as the building block of team play. Many coaches agree – if you can't pass, you can't play.

A pass involves two players – the passer and the receiver – but includes a number of elements which influence and affect the outcome of the pass. The most important element is the harmony between passer and receiver. It is therefore imperative for players to learn to pass and receive the ball early in their playing careers so that they can recognise and exploit the options open to them in the game.

Effective passing depends on a number of simple but nevertheless fundamental team principles.

- The player must be **A**ware of the positioning of team mates and opponents.
- The player must be **B**alanced.
- The player must have **C**ontrol of the ball.

This is the **ABC** of passing: together with knowing **when** to pass and **when** to hold the ball, this adds up to 'reading' the game.

There are six main types of pass used in the modern game.

Hit

Used for passing the ball quickly over long distances, for shooting at goal, and when taking free hits or hits-in from the side and backline.

Push

The most commonly used pass in the game. While it lacks the speed of the hit, it is more effective in terms of accuracy.

Reverse push

Most effective when passing from left to right over short distances, and when no open stick pass is possible. Usually played square or behind square.

Slap

Very similar to the push, and used almost as often. But while the push is most effective over short distances, the slap can be used to make long, powerful, penetrative passes.

Flick

An extension of the push. Used to lift the ball into the air, either as a long over-head pass, or a short pass, or a shot at goal over an opponent's stick or a prone goalkeeper.

Scoop

An alternative aerial pass in which the right foot and shoulder are brought forwards to achieve the shovelling action needed to lift the ball high over an opponent or several opponents. This requires an adjustment to the grip and body position.

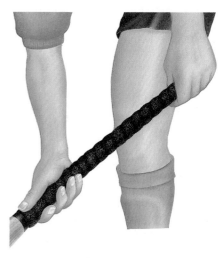

▲ *Fig. 7 Grip for scoop pass*

Receiving the ball

In any team game which involves passing, it is essential for players to be able to receive and gain instant control of the ball. The first touch on the ball is crucial when receiving. If instant control is achieved by the receiver, they will create extra space and time in which to prepare for the next move.

When receiving the ball, the open or reverse stick will be used, depending on where the ball is received and what action the player has to take next.

There are occasions when the player receiving the ball will need to stop it dead. Generally speaking, the receiver of a pass will be required to bring the ball under control and reposition it in preparation for the next move whether it be a pass, a dribble or a shot. Players must learn to perform this skill in minimum time.

The ball can be received while the player is stationary or on the move.

Shooting and goal-scoring

All players enjoy scoring spectacular goals. In reality, all goals are good goals, no matter how simple they may appear.

Good strikers not only know **how** to shoot, but also **when** and **where** to shoot. Although it is true that the more strikes one has on goal the more one is likely to score, a good striker knows when to shoot and when to pass to a team mate in a more favourable position.

All shots on goal should be on target. Saved shots often provide rebounds which in turn can lead to secondary strike opportunities. Coaches should encourage players to follow up shots on goal.

Many goal-scoring opportunities appear suddenly and awkwardly. High levels of concentration and sound technical ability are required to take advantage of these half-chances when they arise.

Good strikers must be prepared to chase lost causes, get on the end of crosses, pick up deflections and collect passes that arrive at different heights and angles, plus control the ball and make a shot at goal, often under pressure from defenders, and in the minimum time and space available.

The key to becoming a top goal-scorer lies in possessing the desire, determination, courage and commitment to succeed.

Defending play

The team in possession of the ball aims to retain possession for long enough to launch an attack and score a goal. The primary aim of the defending team is to prevent the attackers from doing so, and to regain possession of the ball in order to initiate its own attack on the opposite goal.

Generally, possession is regained by intercepting badly timed and misdirected passes, or by tackling an opponent who is still in possession of the ball.

Intercepting

In order to intercept the ball, defenders must mark tightly, read the game and anticipate the actions of the opponents. Interceptions do away with the need to tackle, and often result in clean, high-quality possession from which to launch rapid and effective counter-attacks.

If an interception attempt fails, the defender must reposition himself in order to channel, shadow and close down the attacker with the aim of dispossessing him with a tackle.

Tackling

While the ultimate aim of making a tackle is to regain possession, sometimes it may be necessary to employ a tackle with the purpose of putting the ball out of play, thereby buying time for the tackler's team to reorganise defensively.

While it is unusual for players to employ more than one or two types of tackle in a game, it is important for all players to be able to execute all three main types of tackle.

Jab

The advantage of this tackle is that it can be executed with speed and surprise. It is sometimes used as a decoy to set up a secondary tackle or to force an error out of the attacker, thus slowing down the attack or putting the ball out of play.

The stick is held in the left hand and is lunged at the ball like the head of a striking snake. The right hand is used occasionally to provide support in the preparatory stage.

Either leg can lead, but the defender must stay on their toes, allowing quick movement forwards or backwards if the first tackle is unsuccessful.

Open stick

This is probably the most commonly used tackle in the game. It can be performed while standing still or on the move. It is also possible to make this tackle close to or well away from the feet.

The left foot leads the movement. The right foot provides the pivotal support required to change direction if the first attempt fails.

If performed when standing still, the stick is nearly always used as a barrier – the block tackle. When performed on the move, a more upright stick is used, but it is stationary. It is important for defenders to position themselves goalside and to the right of the attacker before attempting the tackle.

Reverse stick

The game's rules forbid contact with an opponent's body or stick when making a tackle. Therefore, it is essential for the defender to get into a position which allows the tackle to be made level with or in front of his own body.

Although occasionally it may be possible to use two hands when employing the reverse stick tackle, the position of the defender and the way in which the ball is normally carried by attackers (i.e. in front of and to the right of their bodies) makes it necessary to tackle one-handed. The further away from the defender that the tackle is made, the flatter the stick must be to the ground. Tackles made with flat sticks are more effective when playing on artificial surfaces or indoors.

The main points to remember when tackling are:

- watch the ball, not the stick or the body of the player in possession
- time the tackle correctly; don't be tempted to dive in
- recognise when to tackle and which tackle to use
- channel the attacking player on to his reverse stick side (the defender's open stick side).

All these points demand balanced footwork and sharp reflexes.

Marking

Marking forms the basis for all defensive play. The primary aims of marking are to discourage passes to a particular player or, if a pass is made, to intercept it or harass or distract the player to enforce an error, or to tackle the player if he receives possession. There are three main methods of organising a team's defence: man-to-man marking (one-to-one), zonal marking or a combination of both.

Man-to-man marking

The basic concept in this system is when the opposition have the ball, each player from the defending team marks an assigned opponent. Each defending player must:

• stay as close as possible to his opponent
• make it as difficult as possible for his opponent to receive a pass
• retain a position between his opponent and the goal
• adopt a position in which he can see the opponent and the ball.

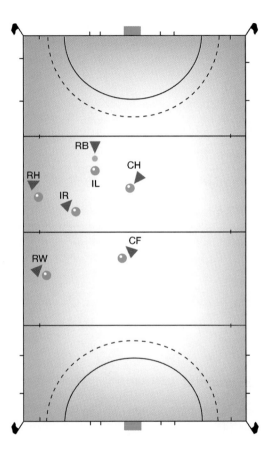

◀ *Fig. 8 Man-to-man marking system*

38

Zonal marking

As the name suggests, in this system defending players form a zone as soon as possession is lost. Each defender takes responsibility for any opponent who comes into his zone of defence. The zone concentrates and tightens marking in the area of greatest danger. Discipline and the retention of organisation are critical to the system's success.

Combination marking systems

The most effective marking systems are those which utilise a combination of zonal and man-to-man systems.

This style relies on tight man-to-man marking of all opposition players immediately around the ball, with the cover defence employing zonal marking.

The crucial moment for the team is when possession is lost. Failure to react quickly can allow the opposition to gain numerical superiority in the danger area, penetrating the defence's circle.

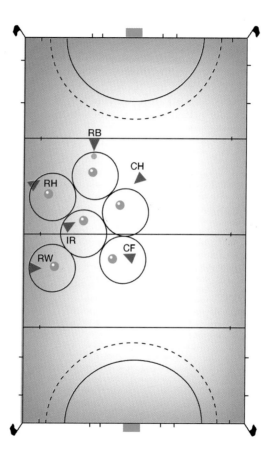

◀ *Fig. 9 Zonal marking system*

Goalkeeping

The goalkeeper's role in the team is to protect the goal.

All goalkeeping actions should start from the accepted position of balanced readiness. This position can be used as a springboard for any save or move that is required.

Low shots directed straight at the goalkeeper should be stopped with the pads. Then the ball should be pushed or kicked towards the sidelines, for safety, never back to the middle of the circle.

There are occasions when the goalkeeper will be required to make saves using the stick or the hand. Usually the ball will be in the air, in which case the hand should be used. If, however, the ball is placed beyond the reach of the goalkeeper's hands, the stick can be used. As with the use of the pads, the hand is used to cushion and control the shot. The ball must not be held. As the ball falls to the ground, it must be cleared in a controlled fashion using the stick or the pads.

In developing these skills, goalkeepers and their coaches must continue to give attention to good, balanced footwork. It is this that sets the goalkeeper in a position from which to make the save.

All good goalkeepers must know how to command the circle, both physically and vocally. They should not be afraid of marshalling the defence, and they should always look to be not only the last line of defence, but also the launching pad of many attacks.

Goalkeepers are not permitted to enter their opponent's half of the pitch, except specifically to take a penalty stroke.

Equipment

Great advances have been made in recent years in the field of goalkeeping equipment. Today there is a wide range of protective equipment available:

- ice hockey style helmet and strong visor
- throat protector
- chest pad
- shoulder and elbow pads
- gloves
- abdominal protector
- genital protector (or 'box')
- padded shorts and thigh protectors
- lightweight leg-guards
- knee pads
- lightweight kickers
- boots or other suitable footwear.

Restarts and set pieces

Every game contains a large number of stoppages. Restarts and set pieces are an essential and integral part of the game and, as such, should be understood, rehearsed and perfected in order to derive maximum advantage from them.

The most common situations from which restarts and set pieces are made are:

- free hits
- hits-in from the sideline
- hits-in from the backline
- penalty corners.

(Other restarts such as the push-back and the bully have been referred to earlier.)

Free hits

In order to derive the most advantage from a free hit, the team in possession should attempt to take it as quickly as possible, and certainly before the defending team has time to reorganise.

If the opportunity for taking an effective free hit is not there, the team in possession must fall back on well drilled routines.

The objectives for each free hit should be known to all players in the team:

- do not speculate, **calculate** (particularly in the defending zone)
- wherever possible, move the ball forwards near or into the danger areas in and around the opposition circle
- the player on the ball must decide what happens, but it is the players off the ball who, by moving into or creating space, dictate what happens next
- keep possession.

Hits-in from the sideline

The same principles and objectives of the free hit apply to the hit-in from the side line.

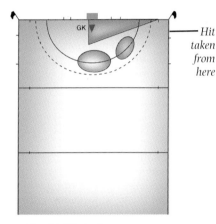

Hit taken from here

▲ *Fig. 10 Hit-in from a corner: danger areas*

Hits-in from a corner

Opportunities to take hits-in from a corner quickly are rare because the defending team almost inevitably has time to reorganise itself.

The attacking players should manoeuvre to receive and control the ball on the open stick side, and in a position that allows them to attack their markers on their reverse stick side.

For the defenders, the problems are different, if not exactly the opposite. Defending players will be expected to counter every move by the attacking side and prevent the ball being received by the attackers in the danger areas. The goalkeeper is the key defender: the team defence should always allow the goalkeeper to have a clear view of the ball.

Occasionally, attacking teams will try to move a well organised defence by playing the ball short and then working it into the danger areas. Defending sides should be alert to this and allocate the task of closing down the player with the ball to specific defenders.

Penalty corners

The penalty corner is a unique aspect of the game in that the rules place restrictions on both the attacking and the defending sides. These restrictions must be taken into consideration when executing attacking moves or when defending against them.

Attacking

Attacking at penalty corners is a matter of good team work, involving individual skill and collective effort. In preparing for a penalty corner, it is vital to consider the following available options.

- To have a direct shot on goal.
- If this is not possible, it may be necessary to move the ball into another area of the circle from which a shot may be made.

The attacking team always has the advantage at penalty corners because the defending team can only try to anticipate what is going to happen.

To retain this advantage, the attacking team should have at its disposal a series of set piece variations to employ according to the situation. The more simple and direct these variations are, the more likely they are to succeed.

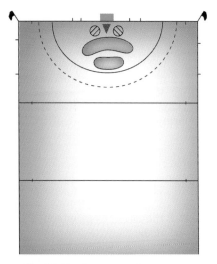

▲ *Fig. 11 Penalty corner: danger areas*

Defending

Only four players and the goalkeeper are allowed to defend the penalty corner. No such limitation is placed on the numbers that the attacking team can employ. The problem that the defence must therefore solve is how to deploy five players to cover all the options available to the attack.

In general, the following patterns form the basis of most defending at penalty corners (*see* fig. 12).

● Player A in fig. 12 runs out to exert pressure on the striker. In so doing, his aim is to:
– hurry the striker into his shot and thereby force him possibly into a mistake, and/or to charge down the shot
– take a line that allows him to play the ball with the open stick, while covering any possibility of passes into other areas
– be prepared to slow down if it is obvious that the attackers are not going to strike the initial shot, or if the ball is passed to another striker

– be prepared to assist the other members of the defence in repelling subsequent phases of the attack.
● Player B runs to the left of player A, and slightly behind. It is his task to:
– cover and intercept any passes to attackers in and around the circle
– take the additional responsibility of dealing with rebounds, knock-downs and other secondary phases of defence, whether off the goalkeeper or any other player.
● Players C and D each have responsibility for the areas on either side of the goalkeeper and near to the goal posts.
● The goalkeeper usually takes up a position covering the middle parts of the goal, but in advance of players C and D. This position may be 2–6 m off the goal line.
● Occasionally player D is deployed in a position alongside and to the right of the goalkeeper, from where he will be expected to cover any passes into an area to the right of and behind player A. Rebounds, knock-downs and deflections off and around the goalkeeper's right will also be his responsibility.

● Some goalkeepers come as far as possible off their goal line in order to narrow the angle of the shot and to exert pressure on the striker. But remember: the closer to the shot the goalkeeper is, the less time he has to react to it; the further off the goal line he is, the more vulnerable is the goal to shots from wide positions.

At set pieces such as these, the goalkeeper is the key defender. He must always be allowed clear sight of the ball. He alone is equipped to deal effectively with direct shots at goal.

Top class goalkeepers feel confident enough in their protective equipment and ability to use their entire bodies to smother and save shots at goal. This is an advanced skill and should **not** be attempted by the novice goalkeeper. The importance and value of using correct equipment and coaching methods, particularly with beginners and young players, cannot be overstressed.

▲ *Fig. 12 Defending a penalty corner*

Metric conversion table

Imperial	Metric	Imperial	Metric
100 yards	91.4 metres	5 feet	1.5 metres
60 yards	54.9 metres	4 feet	1.2 metres
55 yards	50.2 metres	18 inches	45.7 centimetres
50 yards	45.7 metres	9.25 inches	23.5 centimetres
40 yards	36.6 metres	9 inches	22.9 centimetres
25 yards	22.9 metres	8.81 inches	22.4 centimetres
16 yards	14.6 metres	6 inches	15.2 centimetres
10 yards	9.1 metres	3 inches	7.6 centimetres
7 yards	6.4 metres	2 inches	5.1 centimetres
5 yards	4.6 metres	28 ounces	794 grams
4 yards	3.6 metres	12 ounces	340 grams
1 yard	1 metre	5.75 ounces	163 grams
7 feet	2.1 metres	5.5 ounces	156 grams

Index

advantage 18
All England Women's Hockey Association 2
attacking 26–7, 30–4, 43–4

ball 9
    handling 16
    out of play 12
bully 13

captain 3
caution 22
controlling the ball 30
corner flag 4

defending 14, 26–7, 35–6, 44–5
dodging 31
dribbling 31

English Hockey 2, 7
English Hockey Association 2
English Mixed Hockey Association 2
equipment 9, 40
extra time 11

Federation Internationale de Hockey 2, 7
flag posts 4
foot–ball contact 16
footwork 27, 29
free hit 17–18, 42

goalkeeper 3, 9, 14, 16, 23, 40
goal 6

goal-scoring 13, 34
golden goal 11
grip 27, 29

half-time 11
handling
    the ball 16
hit-in 43
Hockey Association, The 2

lines 7

marking 38-9
    combination 39
    man-to-man 38
    zonal 39
match officials 3, 25
match penalties 12, 17–21
misconduct cards 9

obstruction 17
offside 18
open play 12

passing 32-3
    flick 33
    hit 33
    push 33
    reverse push 33
    scoop 33
    slap 33
penalties 17–23

penalty corner 17–19, 43–5
penalty spot 7
penalty stroke 9, 11, 17, 20–1
personal penalties 12, 22–3
pitch 4

raised ball 14
receiving the ball 34
running with the ball 30

scoring 13
shooting 34
stick 8
striking circle 3, 7
substitutes 3
suspension
    goalkeeper 23
    permanent 23
    temporary 22–3

tackling 35-6
    jab 36
    open stick 36
    reverse stick 36
timing 11

umpire 9, 24–5
uniform 9

vision 27, 29

warning 22